Ploughing On

Robert Ramsay

Collected Poetry 2008-2012

An environmentally friendly book printed and bound in England by
www.printondemand-worldwide.com

Mixed Sources
Product group from well-managed
forests, and other controlled sources
www.fsc.org Cert no. TT-COC-002641
© 1996 Forest Stewardship Council

FSC

PEFC
PEFC/16-33-415

PEFC Certified
This product is
from sustainably
managed forests
and controlled
sources
www.pefc.org

This book is made entirely of chain-of-custody materials

The polish on the mole-boards
rises from the furrow like a ship
flashing blindly;
wide and high it swings
about the headland,
bites down and drives,
long swimming strokes
through mother earth,
duty, destiny and life,
chatting with the stones
and flocking shrieking gulls,
on into a fading day.

www.fast-print.net/store.php

Ploughing On
Copyright © Robert Ramsay 2013

ISBN 978-178035-555-9

First published 2013 by
FASTPRINT PUBLISHING
Peterborough, England.

Contents

5

I. Farmland

The grain-drier demands, for the umpteenth time,
I leave this couch.

Every season for us in Scotland
the weather erupts without self-control;
if it's rain it's grey rain and cold
from a narrow all-enclosing lid; or
sun, dry sun, and the wilt –
wilt on the crops and hedgerows
cracked ground.

This says nothing of the light tones
witch-dancing, heart-lifting glances,
nor the soft banks, the moss places,
far glimpses and feather flit,
still sounds from the deep heart
dark water.

From this confused inconstancy we harvest
crop, life, livelihood and meaning;
dodge the change, weave through the isobars
to pick or pluck each and all on trust,
in trust.

Here our overalls are our altar-cloth
each morn our mass
as acolytes we labour, pilgrims we walk;
and somehow, beyond reason,
smile and are blest.

Commanding an empty field
a heron-advocate or writer to the signet;
I see the start of spring buds
a sort of ginger tan.
All the cows are sitting, chewing
sheep stand to graze;
the sea world-war grey shot through with charcoal,
menace of rain.
The locomotive lacks the sway and rattle
of a mainline steam train,
short on urgency, no thrill
no you
and I am divided from the land by glass,
the atmosphere, the djinns.
A gull soaring, free from brain sweat;
barley ruffled, sighing, green yet.

A high bark resounds through the woods
like some Edwardian mechanical device
wanting grease, a pump perhaps, or rollers.

I walk down to see what kind of beast is here
past flowering currant, laurel,
scent honey-toxic, a hawk-killed bird,
two score of feathers left.

A de-stoner precedes the tatty planter
yelping like a caged despairing creature

I amble back, a whingeing buzzard
ground elder
complete absence of any compensating breeze.

Blinky skies and May blossom herds
grazing beside dark and trusty tiles of wheat crops,
England's south set about with teacups
as for a church bazaar;
the engine, somewhat piano,
maybe hung-over, streams us northward
lugs its bones across the crossings into Newark,
Peterborough actually, but does not scan,
it might nearly start to think of spitting raindrops
my cell-phone ringing –

After York, piebald ponies eat creeping buttercup
because they're there,
this far north the sky is closer, crosser,
my empty John Smith's beer-can shimmies
on the table; the farmsteads frown,
I'm going home and raggle-taggle lambs
chewing sour land this nearly June
and not quite summer.

Now sun and yellow rape fields blinded,
ferns beneath leafy sycamore and leggy birches;
the limbs and musculature of Perthshire
covered in a thin green lawn dustsheet
Tay river oozing flatly from the Fair City –
so we miss out Fife and Leuchars,
Sunday maintenance, the river tea-stained.
We tiptoe by the dozing town, its weed
and rust-infected arse,
hold our breath –
all the hills smoked like bee-hives,
pretend a blue — half close your eyes
it might be England, France even;
down the carriage an American
makes conversation...

Oh crivens, cry my heart!
Not a single soul in all these wide-armed acres
not a beast, well a puckle,
a creature called car, again a van,
a lone crow — at last a man!
With dog, struggles over grass
hauls off a boulder, dense enough
to gar him stotter.

The scattered snake-skins
of homo sapiens discarded, polythene
fetched up against the leeways,

(nice how hand-held text-machines keep
the hoi polloi biddable, mum)

The Tweed at Berwick aegean blue,
a stack at the mouth — my acres
out of view, nothing over two rooms high
and the German Sea
I'd swap it any day for Greece,
Allemandal now. Oh, that long long
arm of Lindisfarne wallows there
needing rogered, all of it slack-legged
and groaning for the spurt of sperm,
reproduction's blind convulsion
and the chrysalis conversion,
May again...

A molten sky
seeping like a furnace over Berwick
to the north west,
magma on a summer's eve,
the swallows racing low and looping,
air mild and fragrant, sweet with barley,
I, alone with it, pour a blended whisky,
watch the poker-face of silence
take off my shoes
edge towards the zone.

Today thunder grumbles all around,
more indigestion than ill intent
the sun beats on me with bull-whips.
I de-hydrate and rogue a barley field,
swing through it slow,
burning.
Then comes the downpour,
needed but not wanted,
making its own rhythm, thunder stilled,
crops lapping, swelling.

There are goldfinches flaring, dancing
six of them above the thistles.

The day slopes off into night
and harvest stops;
from white to yellow, mauve,
now sudden blue-grey,
oil black the shapes of twitching trees;
some bird or bat streaking fast,
faster than these old eyes react;
and I am dumb to all that,

The summer smells of sweetness
mixed with corpse are gone,
snuff and spice pervade the woodlands,
still as praying mantises – Buddhist monks
dressed in damp and mildew
this trap more honeyed, the honey richer,
more intense; two roe deer cross my path
at fifty yards and do not know me.

Soot black and oil black
hands, clothes, arms and nose;
barley chaff, awns and dust
in neck back ears and eyes,
sinus throat, residing;
harvest lice and other bugs
crawling where they have no right.
At this time one does not smile.

Breaking, breaking, always breaking,
service this and service that,
bolts and nuts in places hid,
and no spares.
The engineer is called at last;
he hits some things, butchers more,
and stumped, renews yet more.
Just, it goes.
At this time one does not smile.

Before the next collapse
he sends his bill for parts;
one hundred forty three pounds plus VAT
and travel time and labour
at thirty pounds an hour
for seven hours; total 3-9-2.
The ink is not yet dry,
again it breaks.
At this time one does not smile.

The train coughs discreetly with its horn
and willow herb of course.
Yesterday I shrugged into harvest mode,
ate dust, barley awns in boots, ten
thousand pounds of grain hauled to store
in a cracking westerly sun-bleached breeze;
sore-eyed home to bath and beer,
tomorrow more.

A burnt-down pea field glows like ginger,
airforce-grey cloud cigars settle down
for the night in the last pink
of the sky. Trees blacken, fray
like worn fringes to the fields
crows protest that it is not yet time.

The combines rumble, beacons strobe,
the west wind swears on its mother's life
we will cut grain tomorrow;
pigeons flap and coo in the couples,
only the leaves of the poplars
whisper their discord, the flit of the bat
and the last of the blue –
house lights come alive.

Welcome wild Nor'westerly wind
the clouds scud by and reel with the sun
harvesters zing and hearts sing
the plough cuts deep and chocolate.

The smiling chatter of churlish men,
ploughmen, farmers, grumblers all,
now they can work, now they graft
fulfilling their life's role.

Shout from the granaries, call from the lofts,
Its harvest time, hurrah! Hurrah!
Come on the dirt, oil and dust
this is the time the money rolls in;

work all night and work all day
a year's labour is justified;
absorb the thumps and parry the blows
in harvest time (as we did of old);

we the untouchables, we the gods
alive on our land as summer subsides
the fields are clean, the barns are full,
aloof from the rest of the world.

The patina the sun puts on the leaves
and grasses creating fossils
or an unnamed metal,

weeks of rain seem lessened
in this sun, the North Sea swimable
late September. All we losers –

writers, farmers, struggling
up hill, inured against truth by
a placebo known as hope.

The cattle, sheep, are frozen, fixed,
bonfire smoke moving waving,
blind land brims with leaning crops.

The rooks don't give a toss
plough moves on, turns
works the alchemy.

Bouts of straw and some baled,
rib bones in potato drills
blond barley mattresses of fields
and plough.
No dogs, no bulls,
the barks, the roars, snarl
are all mechanical.

Far off the woods
fold into the hillside crevices
like crotch
here nissan-hut tunnels
of polythene, ranked, discarded
condoms – safe farming.

Ratting the Stacks

Nicky-tams of jute and twine
the collie's serious frown
gamie up wi' three labs,
happy as Larry, bleeding lips.

The task is to thresh the stacks of corn,
murdering vermin just a sport
a by-product, an auld way
of team building, you might say;

singly, sheaves forked to slaughter
devoured by the mill with an angry bark,
exposed rats louping, men's laughter,
us shrieking loons swing our sticks.

Plough like bitter chocolate, acres
licked and layered, flat as basements
South Fife worked to perfection,
petrified for winter weathering,
next year's birthday cake
not yet iced.

Hairy warts of straw clumps
the ploughman's shame,
the cottage smoke loiters, rime
in the vales hanging, trees
queuing for their pension
bus pass.

A ridiculous pale blue picture-book sky
bronze-Syrian-cohort light slapped all over
wide-spanned silence broken only
by the whisper of my footfall,
on frosted powder, Christmas eve 2010,
the cold pinching my chest, grips my legs.
At the utter stillness of the beech trees
one chaffinch sings, rabbit track aye way,
low the sun barrels orange at me
from southwest, separates the hills
with blue elongated shadow,
I have no rights here.

The defeated clouds are not trying,
in a blue and pink tinted field of crystals
above a crop of wheat so comatose
it knows nothing of today,
of the horizon sky
stained dirty yellow, southward,
the sunrays warm, with kiss,
my right cheek; singly,
serious pigeons trundle past, what
am I to this, I who'll run inside
to warmth and shelter?

Still frost on the ground at North Berwick
and snow, and snow — a speckling.
It is that bruised liver look to the land,
that drunk's face in a storm, the
beetroot, ginger, Bovril concoction that makes
repulsive this old vegetation, flat and filthy,
glinting and ghastly, a torch-lit
charnel house. The white of the snow —
sugar coating yesterday's slaughter,
the wan beiges of ancient grass
and stubble dead as a twin-set
discarded and stiffened by frost
greens a mockery, chemical from a can,
the dark of the sea a haven— tombs
and catacombs, encompassing
wrap-around shrouds and fuck those clouds
spray-can cream, just as tasteless –
not one soul.

Doors locked
The sun has opted out,
left the stage to freezing fog,
and no air moves.
The striated land comes and goes
trees, cotter-houses, barns –
breaching through;

behind that far off hill,
Turner's turmoiled clouds,
orange light,
a green palate spread about.

We truckle through to Haymarket
glazed dumb citizens,
catatonic stones seep black tears,
nostalgia wrapped coaches
doors locked.

That faceless voice modulating
our very brains' edges –
ping and pong –
and out we sneak, a votive thanks,
one half-digested ciabatta
gins come and go with
metallic tonic,

Kettles' cracked black pepper crisps,
and who gives a fuck for
the Yanks' nomenclature?

How marvellously static the sheep stand
grazing, still as new rape
and wheat,
and does the candle-weak sun lift
the dew, the cumulo-nimbus watchful.
The sea shades are numberless
sleight-of-hand shifting green to bronze,
to blue-black, pure white,
in a kind of ex-public school mock arrogance,
ennui or casual boredom.

Thus we span our land, our home,
our country, relaxed and proud,
on edge, neurotic,
locked doors the mentality,
the elephant we don't speak about.

Those old diesel engines with decompression levers
do you remember? More stubborn than mules,
they'd break your heart
and, jeez, the kickback!
Body language does not work on those things,
which is why women hate them,
you cannot catch their eye.
Machines like this make you remember fondly,
as a childhood girlfriend could,
I can not work out why.

Seven thirty of an evening
the swallows make like shadows on the wall,
pink with sandstone and the lounging sun,
I do not give a toss;
breezes ruffle the trees' tendrils, like a dad,
pastels croon in the upper airs,
I'm drying grain and I don't care,
on the rack of chaff and sanded eye,
a tautness found in hide drums
and near insanity, a piano plays merrily
moves me not, that usquebaugh
my reflex now.

II. Hinterland

Deep absorbed in jazz, brain loose and free from meter,
We hold hands, like kids.

Soliloquy

These passions named as Love are not so.
That word and those four letters cannot hit
so wide a mark, a second barrel is required
to give them sense.

Fire-Love is desire which takes and gives
all, to, from and in each other, blindly,
magnetic dipoles stuck eternally together.

– Whereas that hunger for the whole well-being
of ones focus is called Nurture-Love;
takes nought, gives all of time and passion,
wild sacrifice of ones entitlements,
up to and beyond the door of death.

Romantic love seems to suit itself
wanders tipsy out of all control
mewling weeping laughing shining sulking
drugged and drunken, blinded in both eyes;

but Pure-Love is innocent of passion, makes
no demands, exists, and in that state
we call it Holy – (yes priests confuse the matter)
but what we know is this Love, which fills

the gaps between us like Olympian fluids,
oils and energises life, or to be precise,
me, makes me to be not a corpse or zombie,
conformer, slave; but to join the world free
and erratic as electrons in their orbits.

He stood, then dizzy, sat down fast,
And crouched and lay on dampened grass.
Restored he rose once more to work,
And lifted yet another rock
To place upon the heaped cart,
And on again from stone to stone,
The handy boule, the mighty boulder,
Each was wrestled to that cart.
The wagon tipped and load again,
He works his day across the furrow,
Inured to cold, ignoring pain,
(An this were done, another chore),
His steps were slow his pace was sure,
His eyes were lit with stubborn glow,
And calloused hands scratched and raw,
Guts churning at hunger's gnaw.
The ending day and sunset fire,
He swings weary limbward home,
The greeting collie's raucous call,
The goodwife's silent sweating look.
Cold washhouse sink, carbolic soap,
Kick off boots and hang up coat,
And silent sup and read the news,
A mug of tea beside the hearth,
To sleep in cot without a cheer,

Day in and out and on for ere;
Forgotten life, forgotten love,
Focussed sole upon the goal;
Feed the weans and pay the bills,

London's empty and I don't know why.
Has everyone vamoosed, or just in hiding?
Public transport free of fuss and clutter;
were they, before, all tourists, who
the recession keeps away, and in truth
the Capital is not overcrowded?

But the cars too have gone, the traffic,
was that some kind of magic
by the mayor
with his congestion charges?
They still keep building though, it's somewhat scary,
not having any evidence of where the people went,
and what was done to them.

They keep erecting walls
each time you make a point
they move the boundary;
every parameter you set, anchorage
they shift the sand, the seabed.

The icy certainty from the dark of stars
right-sprung fitness of your inner coil
the face of God itself — all melt
coalesce with the detritus of these walls
where hope recoils

Who would lose their innocence?
Who does not look back and mourn its passing?
Yet we scramble to the tree of "knowledge"
starved monkeys, blinded lemmings
sheep deranged — "tree of conceit
in a forest of stupidity", value shattered
knowledge of the facts, wisdom lost
a bad bargain, poor trade.

Who would not bathe in the river of forgetfulness?
Land on a pristine shore unlearned?
Memory is shame, shame is memory
no road goes back to Mandalay
no road, no way nor prayer — only
only one leaf unfurls.

It's a marina now, gold watches
yachts serried, everything is tiled
the people off feeding daughter's pony;
that council folk-museum used to be
the chandlers, full of hemp and mystery;
ciabattas now with your Cullen Skink.

Against the blackened harbour wall
the North Sea used to slurp and pump
boats creaked in, burbled to the swell
heads down, fishers laboured, fish slid;
coarse herring gulls would pay no heed
shout obscenities at the wet, whetting wind.

Bus Pass

Today, for the first time
I used my bus pass
all by myself,
crivens!

Out on a romp
a yomp from our gallery
to Kings University
Aberdeen

From drawing comic-books
with a ten year grandson
to sophisticated literature
among the beautiful
and the aged

Washed and brushed,
those latter,
and I had used my bus pass

Same poetry, separated,
not by generations
but personality
genetic make up
nurture? Jings!

It all seems rather distant
unimportant,
now I am a traveller
free wheeling;

Last week my book was published
printed, launched
so I am a writer
and have my bus pass.

Time dead in the station
heart fluttering post-meeting
hovers for the railed migration
and no thought.

Ding-dong, ooze out, reined in,
western sun cloud-gap peering
sea tonal, slated, void,
the sheep starting.

This is no watercolour sky
a pastelist's
bottomless; stoic fathoms
weeks of short days.

The loneness of being,
an empty picture full of
not us — not me,
you pivot on a needle in another sphere.

The very light aloof,
untouched by what it kisses, floods;
I can be of that light
in some wood's elusive core.

There is a tone of voice
in modern husbands, dads,
a sort of wimpish whine,
almost a wheedle. It cannot last;
men are not made to function in that way.

Obeisance to some sisterhood
or fashion gurus; Disney world
and children wield the whip;
the spring balance is too delicate
something has to burst
I have known men die,

boxed in corners, silenced
and with no advocate.
They call it suicide.
No! It's fucking murder,
man slaughter, and, oh,
by the way, it was not meant,
they bleat.

Just am weary
head so leaden
eyes bleary
brain is dead and
life boring
taste buds cotton
now its pouring
outlook rotten.
Until tomorrow
have you a tenner
I can borrow
my giro's due then
I need a few now
to see me through like
well fuck you
I can manage
don't want nothing
it's stopped raining
sun's shining
I'll find another...

yo brother
help a fella

44

The rain-splashed pavements of the void
where puppet pictures flicker past,
dead life makes its movement
and words echo uselessly,

each baby gazes daftly back
from its hopelessness, unknowing;
birds busy with not being dead;
existence a major deal,

great expanses that once boasted
sit like paper on an out-tray
watching time, that lumpen bore,
flaking into dust particles.

All those outposts, where scratching nesters
bend stories round their fruitlessness,
conjurers squeeze sweet juices
from schistose-grit.

Do you buy the craik, the rant,
yield to those soft lying lips,
weep for your sad wee self?
Or spit grit into the eyes of those
who plan to drain you,
and make it fact?

Young men jogging, with low-slung calves
rugby tops, baggy shorts,
pale girls in hooded fleeces
crones scuttling
a million pounds of car flesh glisten
in a side street;

tobacco coloured leaves
swooping like departed swallows
streaming from the plane trees' branches,
northwards, over Fulham roof tops
gather in the angles, hollows
monochrome and witless covens.

Barter

In the heightened moments
when we see the Gods as shouldn't
and them knowing turn an eye

At the dark depths of other times
those same Gods peer morbidly,
we uncaring

There is a bargain there
I never signed. You cannot find
my imprint on a deed

Thus I, of undamaged mind, declare
I think it reasonable and concur
so long as, Gods, I get to be —
You know — Deal?

So the hunter hunts to have, not kill
(unless killing is the outcome)
not fuck, though perhaps –
nor cherish – yet why not?
He does because he is.

Is the high air necessary, fat skies
upward inclines bursting at the heart
the panting views cut out of
Disney's world
descents into the damp still copse
click-clacking streets, vibrating lights
with edgy music, inside
a lidded velvet box
on blinding wasteland desert?
With his head devoid of gun

the prey that doesn't pray
challenges that stretch
as far as plastic flow.

To love like that...

Arthur Paterson, orraman
that was a man could spit!
On driech days he'd spin us yarns,
darning sacks
or rolling rope of esparto grass;
we young sputum acolytes.

Our childish spit lacked viscosity,
and yet, let fall some meagre inches,
a mighty suck-back could, sometimes,
return it to its source-mouth, or failing,
like Halley's comet, plummet downward,
a yard of tail trailing; us camped in the couples
of the rafters, above the cattle,

but Arthur
he was in a different calibre,
could spit for Scotland.
A fine shade of tobacco yellow,
pipe-man to his bones, our man we said
could hit a running rat, across the barn,
with spit; a trajectory of ochre venom:
our ambition.

Go down in the place
low in the heart of it;
empty hands in the deep;
meek in that place,
taste of the tones,
surrender your soul to the place.
Suffuse that entirety,
absorb in your bones
suck, hoover its spirit,
devour the place.
Consume, subsume it,
in the give and take,
deconstruction and make of it,
anguish and ache,
languish and love;
go down in that place.

Finding that ball and socket, link,
us threadbare, stripped of purpose,
slack-skinned, the sun can't stir.

There are a score of noises
crockery, traffic, voices,
colours orange, royal blue
scarlet, stained-wood hue;

conversations, mouthings,
old papers rustling, sliding
on the damp roads, idling
ideas bought for nothing
charms on a bracelet jangle

no rippling wind-wave
no dancing belly-laughing.
The slip of an unseen finger
twining hand to hand
hoist, heist, uplift
a trans-continental span.

III. Childhood

The smell of clean hair and wiggling of tiny feet,

Bed-time-story time.

When Nick and I hit the clearing
they were slumped against a tree bole,
J.C. and Tom, one of those silver beeches
that never made it as a timber tree,
all whorls, and gnarls.
Red eyed and whey faced, they hadn't slept,
chewed the fat all night, the fire's embers
grey and weary as those two;
we kicked it back to life with dry bark,
put on sausages to spit like wild cats,
found some orange juice.

We'd picked our campsite carefully
under branches of an ancient yew tree,
deep shaded, leaking resin,
behind the red sandstone garden wall;
we scraped the ground flat, set up the tent,
blew up our airbeds, collected wood,
bone dry cedar, laurel, and lit our fire.
Smoke hung in the place, afraid to go alone,
coated our sweaty heads with ash,
weeping our eyes; the others came;
we burnt our tongues on marshmallows
caramelised to twigs.
Dusk intervened, we talked alone
of pirates and centurions, no sunset there,
light fading in the field below
and some distant radio. We slept.

54

But fitfully, as the insects and birds did not,
no thought of time those crows and hover-flies.
We let the sun get up first and did not wash,
grandson Nick and I.

So self aware I spent my childhood blushing, hiding;
some people don't grow out of that and suffer agony,
enjoy no sympathy, are left behind.
It sure is not the fashion in this look-at-me world
of publicity and bloated egos;
but what do I know, being unimportant
unlike you who must not die.
If we breath slow enough and do not move
become invisible and so relax
forget that we exist – devour the world.

At that time when women's noses
were dulled and caked in powder,
shreds of swans'-down clinging
like fluff,
(They renewed it publicly at meal-ends)
music was played on strings
pot plants resounding.
I was uncomfortable in clothing,
in a manner only Kipling seemed to understand,
affairs of state conducted upon principles,
then and now, I completely fail to comprehend,
social, emotional stuff —

Oh the simple clean beauty of mechanics,
structures, quadratic equations, shore lines,
smells of fishing boats, cry of gulls,
yes, that most of all — cry of gulls.

Tommy's eight now, a boy,
loose from parental ties but still needing,
self aware and poised in another place,
half outwith the family, half not.
"Run wild and loose now, go, fly
step on to the long trail with confidence
a backward glance;
take that lone path and,
with our love your amulet,
be safe, grow tall and prosper".
Yet eight years old.

As Nick is nought
but a spirit, elf,
learning the tricks of the forest
the law and lore of life
working his charms
will-o-the-wisping
around the Juggler at seven
his hands full of us
eyes of spells.

Confirmation of my agnosticism
came at my Confirmation class;
later, with parents and godmother,
after the ritualistic farce,
lunch at the King's Head
and she, a leaping mountain,
dowsed a small methylated fire,
with an old general's soda siphon.

The yellow lab barks for company
and you cling to my hand

We march through nettle and thorn
and you take over the lead

We play in the wood
cross a field full of cattle
You cling to my hand.

58

Flint scarred throat
ruptured sinus
pressure boiling up
behind the eyes,
shiver in a useless coat
burn at minus two degrees
all the spaces blocked with rock-wool
brain-lagged goose.
I'll bet a bundle
Tommy's glad he's not in
school — today,
Granny swaddling him in goose
down duvet,
Yeah.

Low sun blazing
Blasting motors off the road
pixilated puddle-splashed windscreens
blind as toilet windows,
the part-frozen wash-wipe
dribbles like an old man;
this winter enveloping
drivers in thin smiles
and unremitting fingers –

"I'll sing you one-oh"

Shut up Dad

Somewhere deep
under a stone cliff
down a pothole, lies lost
some part of you, forgotten
until this moment,
reluctant to come to mind,
like icemelt,
brittle, azure, emerald,
some discontented peacock feather.
That road is closed, time forgotten,
but the echo rattles in the crevices –

"Hey Jude"

No

"Can't buy me Lo-ove"

No no no.

"Play the game, you cads, play the game"

What!

Be contented then with this wee jewel store,
engagement ring,
all, and more than all
he could afford — your maker
think on that.
The tree's weak smile,
hill's exaggerated yawn;
the sea is trying though,
through cold currents,
that distressed moon,
showing maturity
and compassion in those waves
filled with bay sand.

"Froggie went a-courting, he did ride."

Oh God!

That — the secret optimism
of the young, the shaming;
my drink here in this saloon
of last chance — rum?

I remember clover swards
and hay; runny cowpats, stooks,
single engine mono-planes
bi-planes and scythes

Church services on Remembrance Day
pounds, shillings, pence, ink pens
blotters, sealing wax
brown paper, twine and string

Horse manure dry enough
to pick and throw at sisters,
Irish cattle in hand-bedded courts
turnip slicers, gooseberry jam

Taking the sugar-beet to
Letham Grange Station
into railway trucks to
steam-haul to the Cupar factory,
that tiny shunting engine.

Old women, black clad,
with boxes full of miracles,
horrid teeth and lavender,
whaleboned into shapes of
schooners' figureheads.

Fuller's walnut cake
oh yes, My God, and
that triple layered chocolate one,
how I loved that granny
Mother's mother;

But no! I don't remember tastes
or smells or any of these things –
in actuality
just of them
like bleached snapshots.

You have to live again
that life, not this one,
the one that is.
I won't revisit
retrace my path

With so much yet to do;
but sometimes,
in a summer arbour
or by some flaming flicker,
yes then, yes then.

I happened upon a red squirrel,
Of course he darted behind,
Body language saying "let's play",
He zoomed round about, up and down.

But I can't play darting behind,
I simply don't have the speed,
I can only lumber about,
So I stood and watched from the ground.

He scuttled some more, here and there.
He darted behind, once again,
Then he went, in a flounce of contempt,
And I lingered, admiring, bemused.

Foghorn from the Inchcape Rock, German Sea;
pirates, wreckers, war spent
East Kent, the Goodwin Sands;
The sun bewildered by sea mists,
warships, u-boats ghost the coast, lighthouses
strobe Marie Celeste; me, the child
tucked up, sleeping.

Roaming the byways
no helmet or adult company,
Robin, old, mean and chestnut,
slut Maisie, one-pace, lazy, easy,
dappled grey, ours for the taking;
dad came once, but got the message,
ours to give or take –
that cannot happen now, the owning;
the reins are in state hands
only the sleekit free.

Prep School

I suppose,
crammed as I was
into ungainly tweed,
learning sly ways from the crabs
patience from sea-mists,
the fact of Broadstairs could be not other
than Aladdin's Cave
Edwardian bouillabaisse
of prestidigitation –
unless that was the frontispiece
masking forge and foundry
steam hammers, crimpers, press;
the memory of what I was before
only partly wiped
like the Formica topped tables
in the cafés, egg, chips
and froffy-coffy houses, Tizer
shadowed by that previous existence
I watch now the veneer cracking
shellac patina disintegration
my counter-metamorphosis; bicker
from herring gulls, rotting seaweed.

Those old fireside games
Granny taught us,
Spillikins and Racing Demon,
Dumb crambo and Up-Jenkins,
smelling of dust and moth balls,
camphor to you; the automaton stilled
too infirm to resuscitate, milk
and bourbon-fucking-biscuits,
best behaviour, Sunday clothes.

It was such a harbour, escape
from parental watchfulness,
new rules, new ways of breaking them
old toys, old bones
some kind of magic spell
other world, alternate existence
a secret door to the next dimension
from a sad old bat you strangely
needed to love.

Childhood

I remember the chink of your bracelet, Mama,
I remember your perfume's waft;
the swish of your skirt and black velvet shirt,
and the clack of your high heels, Mama.

I recall your tobacco aroma, Dad,
your stories and their telling,
the rasp of your tweed and the size of your hands
and their weight, Dad, their weight.

I bathed in my grandmother's smile, Mum,
her tongue was the scourge of her time,
but we were her angel darlings, Mum,
and that's where I learned about loving.

When I was seven the girl with grey eyes
and swirling coffee-brown hair,
skin like an angel, who didn't much like me,
it was probably just as well, lass.

My friend who did not quite make it,
I remember his wild happy laugh,
the adults were gone and we were as one;
when he died childhood was changed.

IV. Summerland

Stealing all the blue from the sky, hydrangeas stand,
Mute, in the weed-bed.

Too yellow by a mile
that oilseed rape flower,
smothering the land's planes and curves
in an uneven partnership
with the green bits, like two unmatched dancers;
an overweening smell
puts aside the subtler odours,
mannerless as commuters –
I begin to like it.

In May, this Middle England,
so overdressed in blossom,
shows up my meagre spring home, its poverty,
yet Angus County oozes fatness,
Scotland's gold coast raw
as a green Bordeaux wine,
sweet with acidic promise of "not today",
while, here, buildings wallow in the sun-green sward,
loaf with beer-melt, seepage, ullage,
long strokes to mid-off in a girlie wind
that could not warp your back in agony
or raise, a thousand feet, the screaming hawk.

How much is weed, how much flower
where does law end,
crime begin
bluebells or wild poppies,
wood anemones, pansies?
I can smell no boundaries.
I do not like judges;
so many trees
they make not rules,
so many pensioners, no need for words.
In the Wild West, fence builders got shot,
I like that. The rhododendrons went "bush"
in Scotland, I like that.

I love Kipling, all poets' truth
– artists; bring on those wild flowers.

The plump unending light of quietude
God's arms spread endless wide
private whispers from the wind
insects,
concentrating birds....

Your distress at tractors, chainsaws
innocent in passing but distress
motor bikes, lorries, planes even
garden noise....
and smells, silage, dung
pig-slurry hens
and sights –
how you rail at pylons windmills;
memories
of your urban brutal structures,

but is the vista spoiled
or is it you?
I see past, to contours colours
folds shades textures
the light's moods

When I tear apart in traffic's prison
suffocate in department stores
you glide
blossom in the furnishings
haberdashery
I don't know, whatever.

If you can give me more than this I am gob-smacked
so many bluebells, yellow poppies,
all the plants I do not know the name of,
is that leptospermum, this ladies' mantle?
Crowding in like children to listen to my story;
trees dense with foliage, colours, velvets
and two old men chestnuts naked yet and scraggy;
such discretion, old-world manners,
this one dimension, this my planet.

From the Tay Bridge
Scotland obscured by plates of tin
like Europe in days of chivalry,
a magician's wand.

The clouds are breaking into joy
fields in wet despair
no one in this train is speaking
and I am watching idly,
– for whom or what...
... Jimmy Smith is playing easy,
might think he was watching us
his saxophone compadre flying
like a seagull; azure riffs
The paintbrush rests.

Southward we are heading,
where laws are drawn,
the Rights of Man confounded;
whole communities killed.
We, who call ourselves
the brave and free, watch,
Grappelli's fiddle singing on.

Rudely straight and nearly still across the sky
the utter silence of a vapour trail,
a finger-nail score, that, next time you look, is gone;
how certain, but discreet, the birds' refrain.
Close up, the rushed congress of wind and branch,
far off, modest man-made vehicles go past,
is it déjà vu or groundhog repetition,
year on May on May on year on year?
Even the insects don't seem really bothered
but they live short, die quickly
and we, right busy, fill our worlds with things
to block out that seasoned repetition,
not sit and hear our languid cancers grow.

So many flowers and such blossom, petal fall
as tomorrow really truly doesn't matter
it's the sun's drill that illuminates
our strange indifference to it all.

And this my cry
"Stop season stop"
In that pausing I will lie
and bathe in sun
hot sun and bees
then harvest yes
and blast exploding autumn
strip the trees
halt again to let the old catch up
before the doors of winter
shut for ever
please.

On the diving board
its very lip, curled toes;
so I cling to hard reality;
I know tomorrow, tasted it before,
can manage grind, discomfiture
the strange change of colours
of this routine.

So I cry "and spring
come quickly, stop
this bloody foreplay
ejaculation, time is now"
Then whisper to the moon.

Eight foot girth long dead birch tree,
colonized by canopies of toadstools
midnight blue, from baby's fist sized,
to two man's hands; war medals

on this forty-foot monument
decaying as I decay, in a world
of slender, living trees.

The sun can't warm it now, but,
nor wind shake it...
boy was it something once,
and those fungi — shell edged.

Blossom and birdsong, louder than each,
even the leaves scream out their newness,
the moody wind dancing its purple paso-d'oblé,
and fat grey clouds sit out their disapproval.

The rain comes close
the birds don't stop
the breeze ignores it
branches shiver
the wildflowers sit like cats
one red-eyed bloom peers
from a giant rhododendron
and we all wait.

An aeroplane rumbles eternally through the stratosphere
three balloons on a garden fork indicate a birthday
and behind me its remnants are strewn neglected
jellies, biscuits, crisps, cake and spilled juices.

I can't touch it
I am waiting still
until the wind stops
the light fades
and the rain goes
away.

Blinded by sun
warmed, heated
loose to attack,
mocking laughter.
Made dumb by the sun
unthinking, thankful,
not deaf — quite,
inured though, and
touched by the sun
brain, skin
licked by the sun's rude tasting
fucked by its fast passing.
Turn to the darkening blanket.

What good these leaves now
And me foundering in cold –
Simpering like spinsters
Those coy colours flirting,
Mister-Big-Man light oiling in
With his shoulders, his patronage,
Sucker-punching at the hills,
Dumb-faced clouds craning in
All on all – and my heart sick with cold
In this inevitable flash-warp.

Flat heat of the sun on brow and head,
the chill tug of the wind at leg and sleeve,
song sounds and cry of the birds call,
with the rush of gusts in the trees' tops,
late May.

An airplane rumbles across the sky, and fades,
returns and slowly fades away at last;
an age it takes in passing, holds the sky,
its voided wake fills again with noises.

Spring's wetness cloys in every corner,
the squidgy lawn cries out in green
green lush leaves curtain-wall the vista,
those of my book flap and fret, unread...

String bag
empty like that
and the few things that come run
right through the mesh;
the gulls show some purpose
the station flowers tremor
in the breeze, Stonehaven.

Smell of body-lotion joss-stick,
the sea glistens, ripples like a gong
beaten aluminium, wide and happy
going off to such places
with the freighters, under-currents
remembering depths.
Bison by God! Why surprise?
They were there the last time,
had I forgotten,
that's what we do, by the bucket;
so much land to love
and nurture or leave,
let go like young children;
those contours that foliage,
we'll get instructions.

Shadows long-stretch across the lawn,
each tree shape turns the moss to pine,
songbirds cheer the cold away
to the sun's bleak smile.

They finish sowing potatoes in the railway field.
Pigeons call from wooded depths;
the deep blue sky is like another place,
somewhere tropical.

The shadows slowly traverse and contract,
their shade is chill, reminder to cast no clout.

There is a type of summer daylight,
clouded, not quite misty
warm or cold,
where hedge and tree forms merge
indistinct, yet the outline contrasts
stark on the skyline;
an indecisive time when
what matters takes a rain check
purpose makes a sidestep, duty melts,
love stumbles.

The boiling crater clouds and stonking snowfield sun
seem slightly out of kilter
in this end-of-April greenness
of the borderlands.

How sharply one's breath comes
and quickly the heart pumps the adrenalin tide
when the seasons creak and stir
and one is weather-bound.

I am ready now, believe it,
to pounce on the moving herds,
to battle, once more, the no-can-do's,
in this my Spring spurt, to put my welt on the world.
The soft and tentative shades of Spring are gone;
uncompromising, summer's colours rich;
rhodies, azaleas and, strangely, an owl cries.
Darkness now in this green wall, and its shade
borders on gloom, edges at melancholy;
birds fill the air with a curtain of sound
reinforce the bars of this foliage fortress:

Rhododendrons bloom so still, no air breaths, waiting...
the white-dusted hills of Aviemore
lying thigh to thigh with cloud,
the rest is golden; red, silver,
fawn, green-golden, between the shadows,
stretching down and down,
and no livestock,
chased by this sleek train,
but running out on me and my
blue-brown shiny water,
flowering, fruiting, ripening,
of an instant of self proclaiming rapture,
folds into sleep, within its certain self.

The White Noise was rain, falling
steadily on fresh young leaves;
the intense colours were the trees
boasting their genus, innocently.
A unifying glow powered through,
with the casual indifference of light.

Loose and sleep-leaden,
crops bedraggled, beside
the dozing Tay river,
railside weeds vibrant,
this commuter hyphen
between being and work
locomotive unanswerable,
a diffident Authority.

Endless earth colours
greens, yellow, browns
pasted with convolutes of grey
wall-to-wall, poker faced.
Livestock eating
to live, breed, die and eat
you constant, I a shifting dune,
swirling.

See the cloud hang on the heathered hill
like ague, unwanted lover
sucking at the shelterbelts forlornly
slanting losing grip
its all-surrounding hunger
seeping into ennui, shame.

Jackdaws' "chuck"
hiss of April rain on leaves,
leaves hardly open, nor quite green,
air still, but fresh,
faint and distant songs
so much colour, shades of flower, leaf,
bark, lichen, moss and dull sky;
forcing through and bursting,
the unremitting green of spring.
Veins pulse with life, reactivate
in hope of what, work
connecting with the Earth?
Kindness breaks from the floe and idles here...

Hairy big fly
not a bluebottle,
striped head
not a horsefly
(fit we cry "clegg"),
red nose like a bull,
murmuring on this sunshine day
I think it bites.

I stand alone beneath a brazen sky,
its honeyed warmth is just a frigging lie;
like every mortal soul I buy the trick;
it's rained before and tomorrow's flood is nigh.

Our hearts surge every time she smiles,
her angry sneers and scowls forgotten, whiles;
she only has to touch us with her hand,
and with that hand our fawning heart beguiles.

My brain says, "don't be soft, go use your head"
but body fluids soon make sure I'm lead
to places I don't really want to go,
a slave to enzymes' binding sensual thread.

The simple truth is: I don't truly mind,
I'm easy meat, a sucker for a thrill,
I'll swallow every drink and drug I find,
I know the price and to the price resigned.

And I'm consumed with hunger greed and lust,
and all too soon I will be nought but dust;
meanwhile I jump from ecstasy to hell,
the foolish fluxing of the living cursed.

V. Sheland

That angora jumper, marker of the female world,
Fills one with silence.

Perhaps the sense of sadness
I find in nature's beauty
is love bewildered
compass-needle flailing
that hunger of the spirit
I have for you wanders
somewhere in the hinterland
neglected, but I don't know.

If the pounding thrust for life
for love relapses
sadness is the conservation fluid
tears the skin, the shell
the comforter.

Thin and brittle like a stalk
of some senescing plant
going russet, your fine posture
flicking smile, city girl
from shoes to hair
hides...
behind that dryness droll wit
art deco screen of orthodoxy
what?
Some trap unsprung
distended corpse
guarding a small light pure white
but tinged with...

shivering

it itself protecting one specific gene
or germ, too small to see.

Sun is shining on her cheek
and upper eyelid,
sky black ahead
train trickling,
a routine journey,
sun spills aslant her neck
there is no interaction,
no sign of living but the sound of talking;
she reads a book, a novel,
sun shifts a fraction seems to like it,
stalking as we travel,
skin-walking on her eyelids
while she reads.

Those days of skimpy T-shirts
laced at the throat
psychedelic trousers flared,
white lipstick and back-combed hair,
rhythm n' blues and summer smell
so much promise, a new world —
did it all go wrong?
Did it all go wrong?

Yet the sky's still blue;
clouds loaf in
trees stand cool
the red earth breaths.
You can see her breath
in the frost and the dawn,
days truckle on – but
Jean Shrimpton has gone.

Light seeps away
small darkness pockets
crawl in to take up residence
around the trees and folds
stretch out along the sea-rim
underside of cloud.

The girl with yellow hair
is half asleep and listening to
her head-phones
some men are laughing.

Electric lights turn up like whores,
leaking from the alleyways
her eyes wide open now
are clear and young, but glazed.

Sour water lies about these places,
like the scourings of a teapot,
saucepan and rheumatic.
The ground turns its back
lugs into hibernation,
we are on our own.

The breast-white water breaks
about the cliffs like ecstasy
or ice-melt
death's one eye ajar;
people don't draw breath,
talk as if there was no bomb
no final reckoning,

I ache to smash, to love, to draw apart
and fabricate one pristine thing,
untouchable, transient,
fragile as gossamer,
loose it to the distant nebulae.

It's not so much you're pretty
hair and skin aglow with life,
your form and walk, your smile and talk
as the light behind your eyes;
your humour's smiles off the beat
your temper times unsure,
but your heart, your voice, your quiet times,
the contentment of your sighs.

Dark the menace of those Latin types
arguing in that shaded back room
draw no breath and strangely
do not smoke. Man, the coffee's good,
crudding hot outside, faint breeze,
its warm and rancid breath,
my bald pate stews its bouillabaisse within,
I dehydrate –

An ill-mannered monologue
from each crossing aeroplane –

Seeing some pregnant woman on a bus
this sunny afternoon, her dress
reminded me of you back here in London
all those years ago in '68,
swollen with our Robert, gorgeous
in that psychedelic mini garment,
so much freedom, hope and fun...

The ululating sound
of the female sapiens,
softer than a feather's stroke
can split basalt
break glaciers
before breath is drawn,
to what purpose
or construction?
Castles are built on a word,
cathedrals destroyed on the flood.

Senile joints strung together
by a haute couture thread
false eyelash, new teeth,
straight back, parchment hipbones
clamped, gravity damned to hell;

Another day seen off, breath stole
the hand long played, the broken shell
leans on the fire
flames feeding on the tattered flesh,
dead coral built on coral death,
fathoms high.

See that baseball glove
the one Steve McQueen
had in The Great Escape;
broken in to fit his hand
perfectly, but more than that
his comforter, his sanity?

That is you to me that is,
but just the half of it.
Nor would I change this glove
for his Porsche, Ferrari or whatever,
Bose sound system,
Manhattan sky-line.

If I write a poem
That has short phrases,
Staccato lines,
Like this;
And then suddenly burst out in long and tetchy sentences
that seem as if they will never end, but explode
eventually in one great exhalation of emotion:- then
Will you mind
Or care
Or criticise,
Or smirk
And look away,
Or will you think, as your hair falls loosely forward and
you almost absentmindedly tuck it back behind your ear
with slender, gentle, cool, cool fingers, or maybe lean
back and rill your hands through your waves thus gently
lift your breast, will you think it might be interesting and
forgo a second cup of coffee?
Perhaps not
It's most unlikely
After all
It isn't
Á la môde.

I speak of cheese
Stilton, blue vein
natural mould.
You have a small vein
on your breast, the blue
inside a quail egg's shell.
A glass of tawny port,
with, on an oatcake,
that same cheese —

Your hair is tawny too —
- please...

Does hair-lacquer do something to the hormones,
corsets kill the sense of fun,
mob antics turn fillies into bullocks
high-heels turn the faucet on?

I suppose that mown grass
is some kind of tranquilliser, wild wind
a variety of dementia, happenchance
I have overdosed on that one.

Poetess

You select your words as surely
as your clothes –
underwear, nouns and adjectives;
discard, replace them,
let lie anent rejected verbs,
your tops and shoes;
style your hair – so, alter it
to suit the cadences and rhyme,
pick your jewellery, lipstick, caesura,
trochees, elisions and eye shadow,
paint your toenails one by one
carefully, take your time, deliberate,
the finished perfect product stunning
as a reverse striptease... only –
as your poem blossoms, ripens,
you bare your self, your heart,
the naked verse, your finest hairs.

You may wonder whether this is sexist
but have you considered the corollary?
He selects each word with neat exactitude
unlike his clothing – sloppy T-shirt,
grubby jeans;
picks his turn of phrase, rhythm, flow
don't even think about the socks,
pants – if he wear such articles?
When his polished poem hits the light
I am grateful I cannot see his naked body pulsing.

This dark incense from
the skitter-bowl of yesterday
hangs on the curtains and the palate
staler than smoke-butts,
wiping out your darlingness;

your stained-glass window polished
by a foetid rag;
in the chimera
my hopeful knighthood stained.

Do you know an ancient spell, my Lovely
do you know an ancient spell
an old trick our forebears worked,
when strangers came and threatened force,
or weather broke and wouldn't mend
do you know an ancient spell?

Can you sing an antique song, my Beauty
can you sing an antique song
of secret times and mysterious ways,
of sacred groves and bygone days
which stir the forest's inner moods
can you sing an antique song?

Will you dance a forbidden dance, my Sweet
will you dance a forbidden dance
a dance our distant sisters worked,
that conjures love and other things,
disturbs the Phoenix on the wing
will you dance a forbidden dance?

Will you take my heart to keep, my Princess
will you take my heart to keep
and wrap it in your fragrant tresses,
press it to your silken body,
hold it in your thoughts forever
will you take my heart to keep?

Supposing

What if a girl comes to your room young slender and
giving,
tawny haired big eyed smiling yet nervously yielding?
You touch her and mate in an explosion of fusion's
confusion,
melting and melding, holding for dear life and laughing.
You're clinging like babies but what of your own wife and
children
your darling and darlings at home with your things, your
belongs?
You can't leave them; you need them their needing their
loving unbidden,
but this in your arms is more precious than the breath of
an Angel.

Suppose you're a Muslim then it isn't even a problem
take her back to your home and say "wife number one
meet my second"
and all is accepted because it is of the tradition
but you aren't and it ain't, you're a Christian in the
deepest of trouble,
so sneak out in the night like a shite and run homeward
and leave her,
drive back to your wife and your children tasting the bile
in the throat of deceiver.
take it out on them all, your shame and your guilt and

your hurting
for the sweet little Angel left abandoned and stranded,
deserted.

What if she's pregnant, bears your bastard, you bastard,
this Angel?
You go to her, hold it, it smiles as she tells you she
hates you
and cries as you go back to confess, where you're
quickly ejected,
move in with the Angel who knows it wasn't your
choosing.
She can't cook, like a slut she serves junk-food in front
of the telly
her friends are all weirdoes and scumbags and very much
younger;
so what do you do but find solace in the arms of a
woman,
older, who caresses your head on a breast that's as big
as a pillow.

VI. Winterland

I want to walk crags, ride rip-tides, seduce angels;
Once my cough is cured.

Here, in the full belly of this winter night
I can see for miles, and all is pink.
Fat-faced snow lies distended
out between the trees and coppices
hits the hill horizon, melds with cloud,
that grey fleet of stratospheric battle-cruisers
suffused with light pollution and throwing it
back upon the ground.
      I am pricked out,
a specimen, between this peculiar beauty
and freezing cold, as I relieve myself.
That call that Samuel heard,
and thought it Eli,
Sirens sang to Odysseus once,
lip quiver of love-hungry places

or just my head
playing footsy with my body
and vice versa

It is not the inconvenience
of a big snow, the chill and road-ice;
it is the lack of doing,
sitting in abeyance, could I not hibernate,
evade all this prettiness?

Oh, one can stand
just so much of that, I am replete,
no! Foundered,
and dawn will, no doubt,
bring her pale grey light – for what?

Slick in the night chunking at the points,
the undiluted black cloth prisoner's face hood.
Orange probes on random hunts, this Marie Celeste
of the rails cruising through indifference
on a catenery limbo slung from Carlisle
to Reekie – wordlessly and empty.

Over-exposed

An ice-framed photo of the farm
black-and-white but tinted
pink and powder blue, on glass,
back-lit, distance shortened,
traffic whispers, jackdaw gossip.
On a different snapshot
aeroplane across the stratosphere
grumbling, thinks of sunwarmth.

Rhododendron leaves surrender limply,
drips of frozen moisture
on the bud-tips of old bald sycamore
and limes,
the dead horse-chestnut, part stripped
of bark screams white and naked, like
a raw and unretracted penis,
from its scabby coruscated sheath of bark,
deer-prints everywhere;
My boots bark like dogs
on the frosted snow, I scrape
beneath the leaves, and yes –
the snowdrops shoot,
a wild gathering of geese
worry past.

A strange insistent howl
between owl and vixen
me safe on the doorstep
October not yet half grown

moon absent
cloud cover
air whispering
moisture ticking
that beast gone – or stilled

your helicopter comes
but does not stop
there is inclusion
I put my weaponry on hold
and lock the doors.

After a pair of days of frost
we are back to harbour drizzle
scotch November mist, but not cold
Saturday 20th on the train.
Defoliated tree-shapes – hem the horizons,
flocks of birds,
an unforgiving coldness on the sea,
not hauteur you understand,
more like contempt and self contempt –
but how can you – being off
in the Dordogne, Angouleme
in golden wine and sun?
A metallic polish to the ploughed soil
patinated not unlike old bronze,
Churchill's bust,
the Basin wasted, leached
by emphysema
squeezing out its life-bloods.

We speak of internal butterflies
they are more like cockroaches
restless blind scrambling
within my viscera that quasi-fluid bit
devoid of strength, that yet exerts
upon my spirit, its own weak will;
and I am dragging north
to chair a meeting,
they are all the same

but still I falter.
You my nightlight, cup of soup, faring
in a different way, beyond the airport line.

That wheat braird, hardly through
into sodden mud, can it survive,
has it even half a chance
against such ravages? My limp heart goes out
to those beasts, the cows and sheep
enduring fields like rotting bales;
the gulls somehow seem above all this
belong the seaways that growl
to themselves the winter's length
defy me to approach them –
perhaps they do not think
you will return.

Spirit, life-force, brain,
All leached by incessant rain;

land emulsified
into endless mire;

Fit we cry gutters

Dark days darken more
drive us to a distant shore;

Limbs numbed, lethargic
absent friends- cathartic.

Clods build on your boot-soles
as you cross a tatty aftermath
weigh you down but you walk taller,
bog you down, make you grumpy.
Thin of chest you hunch into jacket,
fireplace, steak-and-kidney pudding,
oh shit! Christmas
suffocating food gifts expenditure;
peesies swinging on the low cloud
charcoal over sodden stubble
arthritic wingbeat; gutters spitting
from truck-wheels, shotblast the hedgerows

The air drops ten degrees of temperature
rain-clouds gather at the threshold
a tractor stops for lunch –
that silence waking crows.
A pale light bathes the southward sky
above the rape field, blossoms tumble
piling in, breach the dam,
winter is now toast,
spring hangs on the cusp
Cherokee lookout
on a crag, stretching time out
flat and tranquil. Rain walks
in with a numbing right hook,
Scotland.

How long can a body freeze
heart at full term stay itself
wait for the damned leaf —
spring's demand?

Oh I am a countryman,
can bide my time have hung long,
since winter, so many score of winters,
can set the carburettor onto idle,
but refrain from asking why? – No!
The world's at full pitch and fever boil;
open the gate, let the leaves gush

Walking the dog at night through stars, alight with frost,
above the lamp-stained haze
that is Arbroath; not a breath but ours,
misting to our steps,
nor sounds but restive birds:
it could be as a sign awaiting
my response my metamorphosis.

Thus I shrivel
in this broad, austere domain
down to my erasure, rest upon the dark.
In this festive recess, the tests are mine alone...

The structure of this planet is different now,
but more than that, the surface,
outside cover is beyond all recognition;
dimensions have been transmogrified,
the new patina bewildering
defies my scale of measurement,
even the land, the skies deny me.
I punch my way back into their souls;
force the confessional, sup at the raw flavours
of creation, reluctantly sweetness does return,
but grudgingly. Can it hold?
Is that what I am for,
retrenchment?
Bugger.

Near Winter
the brisk cheerfulness of sunshine
melancholy cloud-base,
the introvert and lonely fields,
fences, those long gone livestock.

Trains wail, and slap of tyres
on neurotic roads
wakes the dozing landscape,
the bottom five fathoms of the air
looped crow and pigeon doodles,
no gulls there,

no wind or frost, no tractor, plough;
fir trees darken in their shade
broadleaves bare
the cyclic story senile now,
weight of change pressing down low.

VII. Headland

Black light blinds as white, thin air chokes as thick, in darkness
Who can I cling to?

Inside the steady rolling drum
of passing airliners – their far howl
the outer-space-note buoyant,
you can kind of float,
nothing in – nothing out, tethered
on a long line across the loch
down river, sun blinking
before the dawn, pre-awakening
until the first thought is,
from the faucet, let,
allowed to form the crystal,
neither lone nor accompanied
drone-zone, non-worried, unhurried.

Dawkins beware

Venom is well and living in the broadsheets
and tabloid press,
seeping, breeding, spreading into
you and me the general populace,
beyond that, across the planet.
Virus, meme, "vireme", Dawkins
it has us in its sights and closing.

All night I leak gasses
get up several times, to no avail;
earlier, a dragonfly, en passant,
crashed into our cabin window;
perhaps he is one of those characters
who won't be told –

– I listen to advice, from all over
it makes no jot of difference, I bloat,
I pass wind and do not sleep.

Contemporary Art my arse.
One short word to circumscribe
the contents of the universe
and start a diatribe,
a fulminating rant.
Crank up the blood pump,
coruscate the Kant that
plays this trump card:–

The Royal Academy

– of sweepings from the road,
melange of infamy
but marketable –
so –
good?

A light beyond perception was bathing in the treetops
the biggest sky I'd known stretching the horizon
autumn birds were calling, hectic in the wild wood
I was stillness, absence, on the ground.

As fragrance, beauty, magic were filling up my heart
space
mind staying dumb, spirit rising up a plane,
saw creatures freely roaming, insured against mankind,
I felt at one, above, beyond, within.

This limbo-place was shining iridescent with such loving
breathing came so quiet I could feel the bitter-sweetness
it seemed as if all nature was resting easy on my arm,
the distant hills bowing at my feet.

I turned again, renewed, to deep inhale the shittiness,
the city grime, the pain, the avarice and greed
to face the world in hope now freed from all self-pity
a detour in my soul's long road to bliss.

I saw a cathedral, a stained-glass canopy
you called it beech wood

gold fabrics draped, and white planks of light
dust misted

smelled incense, you called it
chanterelle, damp leaf-mould,
moss banks, silence

no time-shape but some vague presence
close-distant and big, yet empty

like sanctuary
you called it beech wood.

Banking Collapse
come on you Yanks
don't falter now,
or buckle to the socialists
just when the world needs
honest open faces,
deep shafts of grit.
What rules? What certainties?
The old worlds stumble,
wail and rail.
Come on you Yankeedoodles.

A puffed up juvenile house sparrow
hops alone across the yard, bewildered,
stops and waits for nothing,
head tucked in and rocking gently.

"What ails you, beastie? Is it bird-flu'?"
The poor wee bugger's dying;
house martins chirp all over.

In the chilly waters
of Scottish estuaries
men drown.
The water takes their bodies,
dumps them somewhere else,
in mud.
If there is remorse
it does not show
on the blind-eyed surface, secret deeps.
The tide moves out unsmiling,
moves back;
there is no dialogue.
It is like a government.
Governments are kin to cold estuaries.

Between fear and resignation,
loneliness and grace,
these coarse-built creatures find
the power source to live, survive,
enjoy, take solace from –
what – a scrap of dust?
But, shit! What dust,
what scraps! – don't ponder...
wonder, whiles.

So we ride the cycle like a bike
round and back,
up and down a velodrome,
but every pore and sense, nerve-end bleeds
out and in like some high-octane anemone
in an electric sea,
a sea we swim alone
and deep.

A Sanctus throb
around old basalt,
flurry of a cool breeze
through white linen,
how can I deny it?

The high insistence
of sea-born gulls,
descent to the surf,
its all encompassed growl,
of course I buy it.

Pierced by the ululation
of those girls
dark calling eyes
all knowing curves,
I think to try it...

Set down on muted
ice-cold dunes,
empty as the cobalt
liquid sky,
there I, there I...

The liquid movement of a steel piston, bathed in oil,
through its cylinder, made by man
to gurgle quietly, sleeking up and down,
has more reality than my hand back easing
on your cheekbone; I cannot figure why.

The shaping of some dumb thing, with sore hands,
in adverse weather, brings new-birth joys
which gold and its spending cannot emulate.

Faking it, with pen and paper,
lights some inner furnace, flues open
to roar the flame of life
way into the stratosphere;

I guess, to make our imprint in rock,
as it were a fossil, is joy enough
for trilobites and man, once, of course, our chromosomes
are satisfied
and that is easy said.

See Kleintzahler

he doesn't make words easy
you have to let them go, relax
let the shapes and sounds of them
the ideas and the images un-jumble.
Take the spirit of the thing
without trying, tensing; not thinking
they'll coalesce into what he is telling
by themselves like magic,
you must be loose though.

Poetry, sleight of hand
how it is with children
with sports
coming from beyond your skull;
not so easy sometimes
with the sentient like women,
Gods -
but poetry, August...

There is some kind of internal weakness
in mankind, a shear-bolt, fuse-wire
or overload inhibitor;
our limbs and eyes still work
but are disconnected from the brain.
It is not a bad place to be, this
infirmacy of the flesh.

There is another place for those,
sick at heart, more like a graveyard
or catacomb;
artists paint it frequently and call it Hell
and fill it up with tormented bodies, perhaps
there is no other way of painting it.
But that cruel place is filled with mirrors
and ghastly truths
images of our Maker's face.

If it is proper living
to know your locus, lodestar
I am dead to drift,
bounce, rebound.

If manly to control
the world around, assured,
who then floats with purpose,
focus, feel?

Iron strength resounds,
but does aluminium
or carbon fibre,
sinew, bone and flesh? You

know the answer,
it radiates about you in a glow,
but let your angry falter show,
leave me confident, relieved.

The honest low-church smell of grass and barley
the crass colours of hybrid shrubs
yesterday, vulgar against the muted wood,
now washed out and biddable.
The sun placing itself discreetly
in certain nooks and alcoves
things mechanical, aware, passing sotto voce,
no-one moves,
the buzzard will not flap its wings.
On such days men are called to arms
fight sparingly and die;
wild dogs pull their corpses
and think nothing of it.
On such days girls appear as blossom.

Dare to pit your brains against your hormones,
let good sense and logic rule your life,
refuse to be the victim of your chromosomes,
have your shower cold, and stiff your lips.

One could give way to one's emotions,
live on instinct like the horrid beasts,
indulge one's private sensibilities,
but, my dear, it would be such a waste.

To force oneself in intellectual rigour
should not mean denial of the senses,
more like running them in a halter
to satisfy oneself of who is master.

VIII. Abroad

These throaty pigeons, burbling from arboreal depths,
Radiating calm.

Hey now ganja maan

How is the day?

                          I see the rhum palm standing watching

It rain plenty de morning

The sun will come

                          The birds spill, singing, cruising

How is the body

Cool daddy man

                          Distant drums, is that you Jim?

The sea is rough

It will be better later

                          I hear the plop of tennis balls in the garden

How is the family

They good thank you, thank you.

                          There is no crash, no Wall Street

How is it with you

Yeah man, very good

                          The ocean gives, rests on the beat, retrieves.

See you later, maybe

Have a nice day Robert.

A loose formation
six pelicans sky cruising
with big beast sleight of hand
span the hemisphere,
in eleven wing-beats, in half
that many seconds,
white clad throughout,
far too cool for shades,
gone and don't look back;

I half asleep and grounded
tumble in their slipstream
like weed.

The sea is grey and empty like the heart,
deep and distant as your heart.
All that surf and action the periphery
the lacy edging to a counterpane
the sky not fussed.

The shore teams with activity, separating streams
a self-imposed captivity, the noise is mute
and self-absorbing counterparts, brief,
half-life fading, sand indifferent
and we are tethered.

Those flashlight moments are internal,
the universe lit up between us; our surroundings
vanish in a high-speed zoom-out
you change the criteria, perspective;
in your hand my focus gathered.

In the several shades of white
below the sun
that is my view south,
lies Brufut fishing town, the bay's end
scenes of half-made dreams, Senegal
Cap Skirring, Guinea Bissau, Conakry
love and riches, romance
adventure, poverty and despair
crocodiles and hippos there,
the long shadow of the Congo, Ashanti
far back and deeper,
beyond the source of orgasm
the blood-black crucible of birth and fear
the green call of this forest's womb
where we are made, veiled
in the several white lights of confusion.

Accosted every which way
by youthful dark skinned white eyes, bums
and young guns on the make
mostly incompetent,
touts all, and to an ancient shape,
tired pattern, broken and deflated scam.
There is poverty but this ain't that;
frayed ends of something serviceable
almost pat,

in a brown treacle night, fat moon
palm silhouettes, the muezzin's strident shout,
crickets, drums, lozenge coloured lights
and ever present wood smoke —
uneven roads, that sense of self
as alien, insects big as bats.

Huge gulls, wings blinking
way out against the mass of dark sea
Kwa-Benzi.

Dusty olive the sea
in cold wind and surf spray
misting the shore
at the crook of the bay —
none but me, not dogs
feral dogs —
bask in my hangover
from yesterday's sun.

Hear it for the doves
marking out the clock in baffled song
"Juju — juju"
Passing the time in small talk
"How do you doo, how do you doo"
Sotto voce in forest arbours,
level heads, anchormen —
peace mantras.

Spring-clean the spirit-store
de-frag ol' brain
                on a hot beach,
                                tropic garden,
empty out cupboards,
                lay all away,
float on the tide run –
                feather soft.

What's left is core,   residue,   a skeleton?

        Naa...
                                it's essence.

Fine sand smoking the returning surf
masking the shell-traps
for bare feet, the race of its suck back
ripping at legs of pale string, veined knots;
salted eyes facing seaward gaze away;
here they totter, safe, defenceless, sole
in a white sun on the chord of the ocean
hanging, hanging on.

That fan-leafed palm, Livistona Chinensis,
architected like a bastion,
living, moving with discretion,
head only, trunk towering
military, Cox's Stack, Dundee,
which cannot fall.

But this one bleeds, suffers
in the white sun, arching wind,
stiff lipped —
the distressed shake
of fronds' ends

Now the sea is muttering
and the cape is lost in mist.
This could be the Irish sea,
if it were not warm,
I loose in every limb,
tourists standing, waiting
for clouds to part, and shout —
Day!

Three great pelicans in line
tracking south, wingspans distended
as their gawky beaks,
flying with such confidence,
you could say majesty,
I bow.
They glide beyond my eyes,
leave a hole to flounder in —
an hour's span.

On reflecting a holiday should be,
by definition, without responsibility:

there is a pigeon in the Gambia
that cries "Haverford-West",
another, perhaps South African,
says "What a catestrophe".

This is all I have learnt from
my holidays and I feel shame
that I know so little of the people;
do I know the British more?

We have many birdsongs
here in Scotland that
I am just as ignorant of.
Now I admit that I was lying

I don't feel any shame at all.
I love the Gambia as I love Scotland.
That is all.

As the spaces between the great limbs
of this spreading tree,
so the twitter-song of birds,
high in its foliage, pauses for
the stretch of blue,
letting room enough for me
and all — like tolerance,
like a passing airliner or motherhood;
and the measured step of surf,
indolence of breezes, open as brotherhood;

a small white moth, a child,
a crow, your page turning,
sprinkler orbiting itself,
vultures slide across the dome
starlings creak, the slow unfurling
of a thought, it slips away –
pink-cheeked Dawkins'
protestation, time itself rocking
in the hammock, the compass's
slack-jawed sleep.

So all is symbol
the symbol all-encompassing
its name not quite Lore.
Why brocade and incense
chants and incantation — ritual?

150

(Here a kingfisher flashes me.)
Why He, not It?
Connect — give of yourself, yield,
wherefore then this word 'Faith'?
Slack-off the line.

They called it omo-machine
our dredger, in Guinea Conakry,
spurting water by the ton
from a twenty-four inch pipe
that was a time.

They called it the Boké Project
the snakes were green and fast
I was young, romantic
their kind of poverty was brass-plate real,
100 proof and I felt no surprise.

They call it West Africa
but I found some other thing
in that long stroke of time.

Oceans make no complaints
they ebb on the tide, draw back
and cannot resist the drawing,
decline and resign knowing.

Eagle-hawks go mute to their final culling
when the hunt is in flood
the strength of the blood
failing.

The mouse caught by the cat
is inured to the brutal teasing
the biddable pensioners do not
go quiet, go screaming.

The seas roll in
and the waters roll in, dreaming
and that light going out
flickers again before fading.

IX. Overland

The fire cracks and spits, we sit in this voiceless lull,
Party aftermath

It's very cold this summer afternoon
swarms of martins, swallows hunting low
above the ripening barley,
undergrowth soaking, ploughed fields
gut-wrench dry.
Come touch my hair.

Lip-ripe berries slobbing in the hedgerow
hazel nuts swollen white as sweetbreads,
that wheedling buzzard alone as I.
Thousands drown in Pakistan who I don't know.

This land forlorn and unattended.
One broken hearted raptor in the sky.

June's last days
Inside the vuvuzela fussing
like angry wasps, outside
a likewise chainsaw whinges on
and stops briefly
for the backing warning beeping
of the fork-lift, starts again.
Sun uncomfortably hot
wind a mite too cool,
cuckoo-spit drops everywhere;
how unexciting sky can be
without cloud;
but how we prayed for it.

Mrs B would call in the milking cows
by name – Joyce, Tibby, and so on.
The Jersey lead them in
head nodding, hips rolling like a ploughman,
distended udders lurching,
but all in their own time

to their places in the byre,
slip the chain bindles round their necks,
give them a pound of meal to munch,
wash their teats, slip on the vacuum milker,
hear it whoosh, chunter, burble.

Sometimes a ripple
runs across a flank beneath the skin,
the scrunch of cud, dreamy eyed
but watchful, restive ears
the tail flexing like a whip.

A gallon or two of white stuff
from each of them
mostly into quart billy-cans
for men to collect at lousing time,
the rest to shallow pans,
to settle into cream for butter,
Or dipping with a thieving finger.

I did not much like milk,
but oh the process –
to be part of that life now.

Oksana's paintings are more lyric
than the silver light she catches,
her brushwork more certain than her lashes,
footsteps sure as yearling roe deer,

it cries to me
her joy of living.

yet too proud to speak to me
who buys her pictures,
round my walls, horses
flowers streetlights rivers,
she who stole the light of loving,
she who has lost tomorrow;
I who watch her in her gloaming
her but barely out of childhood.

Seventy five yards through the ride
to that roundel, from the lawn,
the nettles standing five feet tall.

Both Dawn Redwoods look divine
six foot girths and sixty feet
of height, reach the canopy,
twin princesses in a hick town.

Beside,
that old horse-chestnut hulk,
that corpse leviathan,
sports an orange toadstool
a semi-circle shell
fifteen inch across and
primrose at the border,
the root stump all but gone,
it's crippled brother standing yet,
blind, deaf and toothless.

Air transport.
As through wool
and sterile planes of light –
machines sucking air
cracking throats;
zonked and cowed,
shopping in this metaphor
for dying.

One ear-searing push through
the cloud-base into brittle sun,
from that indifference –
low, grey and crouching
a cloud top you could
break your ankles on –
walking to infinity
blinded, as a desert Arab,
would Sibelius write the suite?
Garbarek?

Because we're going to Africa,
because it's us, and it may be
flying or whatever, weightless
if that airport was the passage-way to Hades
this flight is the ante room
of that other place.

Stumbling random as a tourist
this migrating dragonfly
flounders; it could be us
banging the veranda wall.

So nature is not as smart
as modern man supposes,
it too is searching for its god
or, as they sometimes say, "order".

You and I do not see beyond
the blind light of its iridescence,
pour two mojitos
turn the music loud.

I do not think Broadstairs
my prep-school ever was.
The chalk, flint, mock-gothic
architects yellow clay
demands of the shore line
shingle cliffs candyfloss
scraped knees and football –
detention, merit marks
are pasted on retinas
at night by spam bloggers,
spam too invented
to fill up the spaces
and keep out realities –
sacks of it stacks
imported from
Dakar and Mumbai
If they exist
or did once maybe twice
woven at night
by the deranged
in despair homes
along with politics psychology
economics, woven knitted
crocheted – sometimes
I see chinks –   slither through.

There are ice fields out there
In the wastelands of outer space
dark, cold, empty,
dirty ice-rocks hurtling
where pressure, temperature are meaningless
even movement has nothing to relate to,
void of voids plus ice.
There are marriages like that,
societies, governments,
legislatures − hell!

I am looking at an empty view
of flat sea, flat sky,
pale grey, pale grey,
a grey string of land,
some surf, grey too,
battered by the departed sun,
it lifts the heart
promises a suite of music;
there are families like this
northern towns like this
like an old friend's
last kiss.

Everything shot through with surprises
but sparingly;
the sequined eye-glance from the child,
sudden touch of warmth
flashing moth
elusive odour
taste of spice
even you, even I
eight parts corroded
still can catch a flash of laughter
From out among those asteroids.

If you can give me more than this I am gob-smacked
so many bluebells, yellow poppies,
all the plants I do not know the name of,
is that leptospermum, ladies' mantle?
Crowding in like children to listen to my story;
trees dense with foliage, colours, velvets
and two old men chestnuts naked yet and scraggy;
such discretion, old-world manners,
this one dimension, this my planet.

It is the dark of the day,
the shadows at bay and
the hounds still and pointing;
the gold has run
the laughter is gone and
we are hamstrung, gasping.

Our sleeves are shriven, pockets torn
our stores are empty implements worn
skeletal frames shrunken and dry
the batwings fidget and flutter by.

The trees and the leaves of the branches moan
another year passed promises gone
leached are the colours washing your cheeks.
We will haul up from the depth of the well
tomorrow courage some strength of will
the light of the sun, ring o' the till.

That sense of being close
not quite touching,
burning in her aurora
like a gravitation force –
our emotive parts
dragged towards that side
next to her; electro-magnetism
we cannot touch or see
swells up, fill up the meniscuses
to the brim lip;
that sharp sweetness trilling.

Dark reverberations
of our obverse side,
sinew edges soften in her breath
her eye-touch
true delusion, false reality
centrifugal wall of death
the awful sense of our bewilderment
knowledge best forgotten
capitulation,
that we were branded for.

Now numb, maybe dumb
and hard, even a card,
weak as the skin of an embryo
nowhere to go,
so much to do;

Skilled as a craftsman
smart as a salesman
sharp as a laser, cutting the pattern
what can happen?
a lapse, a collapse
a regret, a tear,
to the pub for a beer
and that said
I have lost the thread.

It's that time again
the birches flirting
April still standoffish
the birds sing roundels
Scots pine hold their gravitas.

Neighbours at their evening gardening
I sneer at leafless cherry blossom,
hybrid flowers, floral housework
exterior spring cleaning.

Comes the smiling sneaking haar,
slope off with him, play hooky
rude games and dirtiness
this is the beginning, the start,
Beltane nears.

The mother bitch kicking at her whelp
nipples sore
"What a crying shame" we say
"Poor lamb"
I'm glad they're not my tits
he's chewing on
the rock-jawed loon
lead burden.
Mind I'd not want to suckle
those tough leather paps,
damned glad she's not my dam
I tell you —
Glad its not my call.

168

The structure of this planet is different now,
but more than that, the face, the surface,
the outside cover is beyond all recognition;
the dimensions have been transmogrified,
the new patina bewildering and defies
my scale of measurement.
Even the land, the skies deny me.
I punch my way back into their very souls;
force the confessional, sup at the raw,
the flavours of creation, then reluctantly
sweetness does return, but grudgingly.
Can it hold? Is that what I am for?
Retrenchment? Bugger.

A sad day because it could be better,
much so; and the sea chops,
small half promises in distant places,
droplets tracking back across the window-glass;
I want coffee.

Herring gulls hanging on the uplift;
by law they are protected;
wheat gone flat in patches, prices flatter;
cattle round a yard — awaiting milking?

Across the aisle a woman with some grapes
titivates her make-up, sandy-ginger,
turquoise blouse; the sea is empty.

Stonehaven passes without stopping,
a pinch of doughty golfers, I smell jam
and fruit pies; clouds might be lifting;
lost my cell phone connection,
tomorrow I return to harvest.

The sea is talking in two voices;
the deep steady single bass note
is the breakers growling,
and the cymbal sound is shingle shifting,
reciprocating on itself;
the wind, of its own is silent,
the trees hushed and forest birds.

Men die out there for some sort of half-arsed living.

The high sun levers up the pressure
slowing time,
brains empty and meandering.
Detritus cart-wheeling to a tango, southward,
and that dumb thing, the human heart,
rises kite-like, snuggles in the up-currents,
dream-praying.

The moors are dusty dry magenta.
Gun-oil tints the warm breeze, spaniels strain,
the beaters boil in tweed, is that a peregrine?
Birds bursting from the heather,
a covey whirrs away, guns blast.

Not until a man has kissed his gun stock
is he at one with it, a true shooter;
cordite is not as erotic as a pheromone
yet pleasures him...

To take down a fast flier twisting
must be a reflex,
"in one solution" man and gun.
Now pass the baton to the dogs,
still my heart,
reload.

X. Requiem

To walk on pine leaves –
like wearing brothel-creepers - on Mount Calvary.

You can feel the coldness
of the stone, just standing there,
the emptiness of the Remembrance Hall.
Is that the point?
Only your heartbeat
thinned out past a whisper
beyond the last breath,
an attempt to catch oblivion?
More like numbed respect,
duty, guilt?
The almost empty balcony
from which the gods look down,
watchmen judges.

Uncle Jack's not here,
way out in First World mud
still hanging on the barb,
loved but never reconciled.

174

Whiteout.

Shrouded shapes, that once were trees,
anchor-point the endless whiteness;
grey on grey the feathers fall –
quickly brick and rock surrender.

Chill they howl, the drifting swirls;
softly lisping land the crystals;
lost, we look to find our frame,
our reference points receding quickly.

Now, breathing in a different manner,
giddy brain cells spinning loosely,
we wander in our hopeless quest
for something we no longer value.

Lavinia
You had a great laugh
pealing from your epicentre
– yes, and style
bull–shit you would say
an impatient cigarette–ash flick,

but no –
style, or as you might prefer,
chutzpah, could command a room,
with a sweeping judgement. I remember
I bit your forearm once, thinking
"this is strangely pleasant"
you had, I recall,
rubbed my face with toast
God knows why.

But siblings are tangled up
with tonnages of nonsenses
our internecine fights
and battles with the outside world alike
somehow fitting, bespoke tailoring
We all part of each other one,
part strangers, part regiment –

and then the uncalled for cancer –
I had admired your home-making,
your post-marital struggling
in London's west end,
then Nerja, Spain,
through cluster-headaches, dogged
by recessions yet and fighting,
reduced to the menial at times,

found the strength to make Daisy blossom
keeping the death-march private
living, laughing until that final moment,
and now a tree, copper beech

somehow I think
you would have found that –
hilarious.

Walls keep being built,
each time you make a point
the boundaries are moved;
every parameter you set, anchorage
the sand gets shifted, the seabed.

The icy certainty from the dark of the stars
right-sprung fitness of your inner coil
the face of God itself − all melt
coalesce with the detritus of these walls
where hope recoils

Who would lose their innocence?
Who does not look back and mourn its passing?
Yet we scramble to the tree of "knowledge"
as starved monkeys, blinded lemmings
sheep deranged − "tree of conceit
in a forest of stupidity", value shattered
knowledge of the facts, wisdom lost
a bad bargain, poor trade.

Who would not bathe in the river of forgetfulness?
Land on a pristine shore unlearned?
Memory is shame, shame is memory
no road goes back to Mandalay
no road, no way nor prayer − only
only one leaf unfurls

I remember not the war
but, yes, the sound, the wail of sirens
maybe just factory shift change
or a call to lifeboat crews
but it chilled the blood, signalling
Germans, air-raids, doodlebugs
I don't know what, but fear,
rationing and the wounded,
down-to-earthiness of the mothers
bereft of sons, things not said –
an ex-prisoner of war
"You have no idea what anger is!"
And the ghost
ghost of a sense of brotherhood
slipping off...

This diluted heart
courage leached out and thinning, like hair,
trickle-discharged musculature, shrunken breath,
pale, vapid, narrow,
emasculated skeletal, decayed, unwanted form
vamoose, leave and rapidly
let stay that other we don't speak about,
that grinning mattress,
kelp on the Sargasso Sea,
cloud build and cumulous — that light,
that fucking light
which us anneals, blesses, encapsulates
and elopes with...

Caressing, gently touching, window glued
Two slugs mating,

Long clouds ooze into a silver glow.

As you drive off in the afternoon murk,
Small hand, small wave,

Under the woodland's skirt, snowdrops white as death.